CW01281678

Urban Foraging:

A Beginner's Guide to Wild Edibles in the City

Discover, Harvest, and Prepare Nature's Bounty in Urban Landscapes for Sustainable Living

Alessio rocchI

Table of Contents

Introduction: Why Urban Foraging Matters

A compelling overview of urban foraging, exploring its benefits for sustainability, self-sufficiency, and reconnecting with nature in the city. This section introduces readers to the joy and practicality of harvesting wild edibles in urban spaces.

Chapter 1: The Basics of Urban Foraging

An introduction to the core principles of foraging, including ethical considerations, safety tips, and understanding local regulations. Readers will learn how to forage responsibly and build confidence in identifying safe areas to gather food.

Chapter 2: Tools of the Trade

A practical guide to essential tools and equipment, from field guides and apps to containers and gloves. This chapter helps beginners equip themselves for a successful foraging journey.

Chapter 3: Understanding Urban Ecosystems

An exploration of the diverse ecosystems in cities, such as parks, abandoned lots, and riverbanks. Readers will discover how these areas provide a surprising abundance of edible plants and fungi.

Chapter 4: Top Wild Edibles Found in Cities

A detailed guide to common edible plants and fungi, complete with descriptions, photos, and tips for safe identification. Examples include dandelions, plantains, wild garlic, and more.

Chapter 5: Seasonal Foraging: What to Look For and When

A month-by-month breakdown of urban foraging opportunities. This chapter teaches readers how to align their efforts with nature's calendar for optimal harvests.

Chapter 6: Avoiding Danger: Poisonous Lookalikes and Contaminated Areas

Critical advice on how to avoid toxic plants and fungi, as well as how to identify and avoid areas with potential contamination from pollutants or chemicals.

Chapter 7: Harvesting and Storing Your Finds

Step-by-step instructions for ethically harvesting wild edibles and best practices for cleaning, preserving, and storing them to maximize freshness and usability.

Chapter 8: Simple Recipes with Urban Foraged Ingredients

A collection of easy, delicious recipes that highlight the unique flavors of wild edibles. From teas and salads to pestos and stir-fries, this chapter inspires readers to incorporate foraged foods into everyday meals.

Chapter 9: Building Community Through Urban Foraging

Tips for connecting with other foragers, participating in foraging walks, and building a local network. This chapter emphasizes the social and cultural benefits of urban foraging.

Chapter 10: Beyond Food: Foraging for Medicine and Crafting

An exploration of non-edible uses for wild plants, including natural remedies and crafting materials, expanding the utility of urban foraging.

Conclusion: Becoming an Urban Forager

A motivational wrap-up encouraging readers to embrace urban foraging as a lifestyle. This chapter recaps the key takeaways and provides additional resources for continuing their foraging journey.

Appendices

Introduction: Why Urban Foraging Matters

For centuries, humanity has thrived by living off the land, relying on nature's abundance to meet our basic needs for food, medicine, and even shelter. Yet, as cities expanded and industrialization reshaped the landscape, our connection to nature diminished. Today, in the sprawling urban jungles of glass, steel, and concrete, many of us rarely pause to consider the natural world that quietly endures alongside us. This is where urban foraging comes in—a practice that not only reconnects us to the environment but also challenges us to reimagine the possibilities of modern living. Urban foraging is more than a hobby; it is a lifestyle, a philosophy, and an act of rebellion against waste and excess.

A Forgotten Skill Reimagined

The art of foraging is as old as humanity itself. Before agriculture, foraging was our primary means of sustenance, and the knowledge of edible plants, fruits, and fungi was passed down through generations. However, in recent history, industrial food systems have made this skill seem obsolete. Packaged goods, fast food chains, and supermarkets now dominate our food supply, creating a world where everything is conveniently available but often at a high cost—to the environment, to our health, and to our wallets.

Urban foraging is a modern response to these issues, offering a sustainable alternative to the status quo. It is about reclaiming that lost connection to our natural surroundings, even in the heart of the city. By identifying, harvesting, and using wild edible plants and fungi that grow in urban environments, we not only reduce waste but also foster a sense of independence and resilience.

A Sustainable Solution in a Challenging Era

In an age of environmental crises, from climate change to deforestation, the importance of sustainable living cannot be overstated. Urban foraging is a direct and impactful way to contribute to sustainability. Foraging requires no pesticides, fertilizers, or industrial farming practices; it simply leverages the existing resources in our local environment. By gathering food that would otherwise go unnoticed or be discarded, urban foragers help to minimize food waste and reduce the demand for mass-produced goods.

Moreover, foraging promotes biodiversity by encouraging people to value and protect wild plants. Many of the species commonly harvested by urban foragers, such as dandelions and nettles, are considered "weeds" and are often removed in landscaping efforts. Recognizing the nutritional and ecological value of these plants can shift societal attitudes, fostering a greater appreciation for the natural world.

A Healthier Way of Eating

The nutritional benefits of foraged foods are another compelling reason to embrace urban foraging. Many wild plants are nutrient-dense, offering higher levels of vitamins, minerals, and antioxidants than their cultivated counterparts. For example, wild greens like purslane and lamb's quarters are packed with omega-3 fatty acids and essential nutrients, making them valuable additions to any diet.

Urban foraging also encourages mindfulness about what we consume. Instead of relying on heavily processed foods laden with preservatives and additives, foragers develop a deeper understanding of the origins and properties of their meals. This practice fosters a healthier relationship with food, where each bite carries a story of discovery and connection.

A Gateway to Self-Sufficiency

In uncertain times, the ability to source your own food is an empowering skill. Urban foraging equips individuals with the knowledge and confidence to navigate challenges like food shortages, inflation, or supply chain disruptions. While it may not replace a full grocery list, foraging can significantly supplement one's diet, reducing reliance on external systems.

Beyond practical benefits, foraging also nurtures a mindset of resourcefulness. It teaches us to see potential in what might otherwise be overlooked—a patch of clover on a sidewalk, a cluster of berries in an overgrown lot, or wild garlic sprouting along a park trail. This shift in perspective can be transformative, encouraging creativity and resilience in other areas of life.

A Deeper Connection to Nature

One of the most profound aspects of urban foraging is its ability to reconnect us with the natural world. In cities, it is easy to feel removed from nature, surrounded by towering buildings, paved streets, and the constant hum of traffic. Yet, the natural world is always present, often in unexpected places.

When you start foraging, you begin to notice the green spaces that you might have previously ignored. A walk through the park becomes an opportunity to spot edible mushrooms; a vacant lot transforms into a treasure trove of wild herbs. This heightened awareness fosters a sense of wonder and gratitude, reminding us that nature persists even in the most urbanized settings.

Foraging also deepens our understanding of seasonal rhythms. Unlike the homogenized offerings of supermarkets, wild edibles are tied to specific times of the year. This seasonal availability encourages us to eat in harmony with nature's cycles, fostering a greater appreciation for the ebb and flow of the natural world.

Urban Foraging as a Community Builder

While foraging can be a solitary pursuit, it also has the power to bring people together. Community foraging walks, workshops, and online groups have grown in popularity, providing opportunities for individuals to share knowledge, experiences, and resources. These gatherings create a sense of camaraderie and collective purpose, as participants bond over a shared appreciation for the natural world.

In many ways, urban foraging is a form of activism, challenging the disconnect between humans and the environment. By teaching others how to forage, you contribute to a ripple effect of awareness and action, inspiring more people to adopt sustainable practices.

Challenging Assumptions and Stereotypes

Urban foraging also challenges preconceived notions about city living. Cities are often seen as devoid of nature, characterized instead by pollution, noise, and overpopulation. However, urban foragers reveal a different reality—one where nature thrives in surprising ways. From wild fruit trees lining sidewalks to edible weeds growing in cracks, cities are full of untapped potential for those willing to look.

This practice also confronts the stigma associated with foraging, which some view as an act of desperation or poverty. In truth, foraging is an intentional choice that reflects creativity, resourcefulness, and a commitment to sustainability. By normalizing urban foraging, we can shift societal attitudes and celebrate it as a valuable skill and lifestyle.

Rediscovering Lost Knowledge

Incorporating urban foraging into daily life is also an act of cultural preservation. Across the world, indigenous communities and traditional societies have long relied on wild plants and fungi for food, medicine, and rituals. Unfortunately, much of this knowledge has been lost or marginalized due to colonization and modernization.

By learning to forage, we honor these traditions and keep them alive. This process often involves studying historical texts, consulting with experts, and engaging with local communities to rediscover the wisdom of our ancestors. In doing so, urban foraging becomes more than a personal journey—it is a way of reclaiming and celebrating cultural heritage.

The Joy of Discovery

Perhaps the most compelling reason to embrace urban foraging is the simple joy it brings. There is something deeply satisfying about finding your own food in the wild, turning an ordinary walk into a treasure hunt. Each discovery feels like a small victory, a reminder of the abundance that surrounds us.

This joy extends beyond the act of foraging itself. Preparing a meal with foraged ingredients adds a layer of meaning and connection to the food we eat. It's not just about sustenance; it's about storytelling, creativity, and a sense of accomplishment.

Foraging also invites us to slow down and be present. In a fast-paced world, the act of observing, identifying, and harvesting wild plants requires mindfulness and patience. This meditative quality makes foraging a form of self-care, offering mental and emotional benefits alongside its practical rewards.

A Skill for Everyone

One of the beautiful aspects of urban foraging is its accessibility. You don't need expensive equipment or prior experience to get started; all you need is curiosity and a willingness to learn. Whether you live in a bustling metropolis or a quieter urban area, opportunities for foraging are everywhere.

Urban foraging is also an inclusive practice, open to people of all ages, backgrounds, and abilities. Families can turn it into a fun educational activity for children, teaching them about plants, ecosystems, and sustainability. Older adults can use it as a way to stay active and engaged with their surroundings. No matter who you are, foraging offers a chance to connect with nature and your community in meaningful ways.

This introduction sets the stage for exploring the rich and rewarding world of urban foraging. From its environmental benefits to its ability to foster resilience and joy, urban foraging is a practice that resonates deeply in today's world. Through this book, you will discover how to harness its potential, transforming your relationship with food, nature, and your city.

Chapter 1: The Basics of Urban Foraging

Urban foraging might seem like a novel idea, but it's deeply rooted in humanity's history. At its core, foraging is about finding and utilizing the natural resources that grow abundantly around us. When practiced in urban settings, it becomes a creative and resourceful way to engage with the environment, turning overlooked spaces into opportunities for discovery and nourishment. Before diving into the practical aspects of urban foraging, it's important to understand the foundational principles that make this practice both rewarding and sustainable.

Understanding Urban Foraging

Urban foraging is the practice of identifying and harvesting edible plants, fruits, nuts, seeds, and fungi in city environments. Unlike rural foraging, which often involves vast natural landscapes, urban foraging focuses on smaller, often fragmented green spaces such as parks, gardens, alleys, and even cracks in the sidewalk. These overlooked areas are often teeming with life, offering a surprising variety of edible treasures.

At its heart, urban foraging is about observation and resourcefulness. It requires a shift in perspective, where everyday walks through the city transform into explorations of edible potential. What may initially seem like weeds or decorative plants can reveal themselves as rich sources of nutrition when viewed through the lens of foraging.

Ethics and Responsibility in Urban Foraging

One of the first and most important principles of urban foraging is practicing it ethically and responsibly. While it can be exciting to discover free food growing in unexpected places, foraging comes with responsibilities to the environment, other foragers, and the community.

1. Harvest with Care

Always forage in a way that minimizes harm to the plant or its ecosystem. For perennial plants, avoid uprooting the entire plant and instead take only what you need, leaving plenty for regeneration. For annual plants or those that reproduce through seeds, ensure you're not depleting the plant's ability to propagate.

2. Respect Local Regulations

Different cities have different rules regarding foraging in public spaces. Some parks and green areas may prohibit the removal of plants, while others encourage it to manage invasive species.

Research local laws and guidelines before foraging to ensure you're acting within legal boundaries.

3. Avoid Overharvesting

Urban spaces are often shared by many people, including other foragers. Avoid stripping an area of its resources, as this can impact the availability of food for others and for local wildlife. A good rule of thumb is to take no more than 10% of what's available in a given area.

4. Be Mindful of Contamination

Urban environments can expose plants to contaminants such as pesticides, herbicides, heavy metals, and pollutants from traffic or industrial activity. Always assess the safety of the foraging site and avoid areas near busy roads, construction sites, or treated lawns.

Safety First: Identifying Edible Plants

One of the most crucial skills in urban foraging is the ability to accurately identify edible plants. Mistakes can be dangerous, as some toxic plants closely resemble edible ones. Developing a solid foundation in plant identification is essential for both safety and success.

1. Learn the Lookalikes

Many edible plants have toxic doppelgängers. For example, wild garlic can resemble lily of the valley, which is poisonous. Invest in a reliable field guide or use reputable apps to help identify plants accurately. Pay attention to specific details like leaf shape, flower color, and growth patterns.

2. Use All Your Senses

While sight is the primary sense for identifying plants, don't overlook the importance of touch, smell, and even taste (but only after confirming safety). Many plants have distinctive textures or aromas that can aid in identification. For example, wild mint has a characteristic minty smell, while nettles have a recognizable sting.

3. Start with Easy-to-Identify Plants

If you're new to foraging, begin with plants that are easy to identify and have no toxic lookalikes. Dandelions, chickweed, and purslane are excellent starting points. These common urban plants are not only nutritious but also forgiving for beginners.

4. Take Your Time

Never rush the identification process. If you're unsure about a plant, err on the side of caution and leave it behind. Confidence in identification comes with practice and patience.

Where to Forage in the City

Cities are filled with potential foraging spots, though some are more suitable than others. Knowing where to look is half the battle.

1. Public Parks and Green Spaces

Parks often have diverse plant life and are a great place to start foraging. Look for areas with less foot traffic to avoid contamination and overharvesting.

2. Community Gardens

Some community gardens allow foraging, particularly if they have wild or invasive plants that need managing. Always ask for permission before harvesting in these spaces.

3. Abandoned Lots and Alleyways

While unconventional, abandoned lots can be rich in wild edibles. Exercise caution and ensure the area is free from contaminants before foraging.

4. Your Own Backyard

If you have access to a yard or garden, consider starting your foraging journey there. Many edible plants, such as clover or plantain, grow naturally in residential areas.

The Tools of Urban Foraging

While foraging requires minimal equipment, a few key tools can make the experience safer and more enjoyable.

1. A Reliable Field Guide

A well-illustrated field guide is an indispensable tool for plant identification. Look for guides specific to your region for the most accurate information.

2. Gloves

Gloves protect your hands from thorny plants, stinging nettles, or any potential contaminants.

3. Scissors and Shears

These tools make harvesting easier and more precise, helping you avoid unnecessary damage to the plant.

4. A Basket or Cloth Bag

Avoid using plastic bags, as they can cause delicate plants to wilt quickly. Instead, opt for a breathable basket or cloth bag.

5. Notebook or App

Keeping a record of your foraging finds helps you track locations, seasons, and successful harvests. Many apps also offer identification tools and community forums.

Common Edible Plants in Urban Areas

Urban environments are home to a surprising variety of edible plants. Below are a few common examples to look for as you begin your foraging journey:

1. Dandelions

Every part of the dandelion is edible, from its flowers to its roots. The leaves make a nutritious addition to salads, while the roots can be roasted for a coffee substitute.

2. Plantain

Not to be confused with the banana-like fruit, plantain is a common weed with edible leaves and seeds. It's also known for its medicinal properties.

3. Wild Garlic

Wild garlic's pungent aroma makes it easy to identify. Its leaves, flowers, and bulbs are all edible, offering a versatile ingredient for cooking.

4. Purslane

This succulent plant is rich in omega-3 fatty acids and has a pleasant, tangy flavor. It's often found in sidewalk cracks and gardens.

5. Chickweed

A tender green with a mild taste, chickweed is an excellent addition to salads or sautéed dishes. It's also high in vitamins and minerals.

The Rewards of Urban Foraging

Urban foraging offers more than just food; it provides a sense of accomplishment, connection, and discovery. As you hone your skills, you'll begin to see your city in a new light, recognizing the abundance that exists in even the most unexpected places. While the practice requires knowledge and care, the rewards far outweigh the effort, making urban foraging a valuable and enriching pursuit for anyone willing to embrace it.

Chapter 2: Tools of the Trade

Foraging is one of the simplest and most accessible ways to connect with nature, requiring little more than curiosity and a willingness to explore. However, having the right tools can elevate your experience, making the process safer, more efficient, and ultimately more enjoyable. In this chapter, we will delve into the essential gear and resources that every urban forager should consider. From field guides to harvesting tools, each item serves a specific purpose in helping you navigate the rich world of urban foraging.

Why Tools Matter

While foraging is often portrayed as a spontaneous activity requiring nothing but your hands, the reality of urban foraging can be more complex. Tools not only enhance your ability to identify and harvest plants but also protect you and the environment from harm. For example, a good pair of gloves can shield your hands from thorny plants or potential contaminants, while a quality field guide ensures that you're identifying species correctly, avoiding both mistakes and potential risks.

Having the right tools can also make your foraging trips more efficient. Carrying appropriate storage containers, for instance, helps preserve the freshness of your finds. In addition, some tools can open up opportunities to forage in areas that might otherwise seem inaccessible, such as using pruners to reach higher branches or a digging stick to extract roots. With the right preparation, urban foraging becomes a streamlined and rewarding experience.

Essential Tools for Urban Foraging

Let's explore the tools that every urban forager should consider, from absolute essentials to optional extras that can enhance your practice.

1. Field Guides and Identification Apps

Accurate plant identification is the cornerstone of safe and successful foraging. A reliable field guide or identification app can make all the difference, especially for beginners.

- **Field Guides:** Choose a guide tailored to your region. A good field guide includes clear, high-quality images of plants in various stages of growth, along with descriptions of their features, habitats, and edible parts. Some popular guides also provide warnings about toxic lookalikes, which are crucial for safety.

- *Recommended Field Guides:*
  - "Peterson Field Guide to Edible Wild Plants"
  - "Edible Wild Plants: Wild Foods from Dirt to Plate" by John Kallas
- **Identification Apps:** For tech-savvy foragers, apps like PictureThis or iNaturalist can be invaluable. These apps use AI to help identify plants based on photos and provide additional information about their uses and habitats. However, always cross-reference app results with a reliable field guide to ensure accuracy.

2. Gloves

Urban environments often present unique challenges, including thorny plants, stinging nettles, or the occasional piece of litter. A durable pair of gloves can protect your hands from scrapes, cuts, and irritation while foraging.

- **Types of Gloves:**
  - Lightweight gardening gloves for general use.
  - Heavy-duty gloves for handling thorny or spiky plants.
- **Tips:** Look for gloves with a snug fit to maintain dexterity and ensure you can still handle delicate plants.

3. Harvesting Tools

Harvesting tools make the process of gathering plants more efficient and less damaging to the environment. The right tool ensures clean cuts, minimizes harm to the plant, and preserves its ability to regrow.

- **Pruners and Shears:** Essential for cutting stems, branches, or tough leaves. Opt for compact, lightweight models that are easy to carry.
- **Scissors:** Perfect for snipping herbs, flowers, and smaller plants.
- **Trowels or Digging Sticks:** Useful for extracting roots such as wild garlic or dandelion. A small, portable trowel is ideal for urban foraging, where discretion might be necessary.

4. Storage Containers

Once you've harvested your finds, proper storage is key to preserving their freshness and quality.

- **Baskets:** Traditional wicker baskets are not only aesthetic but also allow air circulation, keeping plants fresh during longer foraging trips.
- **Cloth Bags:** Lightweight and easy to carry, cloth bags are

perfect for foraging leafy greens and small plants.
- **Plastic or Glass Containers:** For more delicate items like berries or flowers, rigid containers offer protection from crushing.
- **Paper Bags:** Ideal for mushrooms, as they prevent moisture buildup that could lead to spoilage.

5. Notebook and Pen

Keeping a record of your foraging trips can be immensely valuable. Use a notebook to jot down locations, plant descriptions, and seasonal observations. Over time, this personal database becomes a powerful resource for planning future foraging expeditions.

- **Digital Alternatives:** If you prefer, use a note-taking app on your smartphone. Some apps, like Evernote, allow you to organize notes with photos and geotags for added convenience.

6. A Backpack

A sturdy backpack is essential for carrying all your tools and collected items. Look for one with multiple compartments to keep your gear organized and easily accessible.

- **Features to Look For:**
    - Water-resistant material to protect your tools and finds.
    - Adjustable straps for comfort during long foraging trips.
    - Side pockets for water bottles or field guides.

Optional Tools for Enhanced Foraging

Once you've mastered the basics, consider adding these optional tools to your kit for a more advanced foraging experience.

1. Magnifying Glass

A magnifying glass can help you examine small details on plants, such as leaf veins or tiny flowers, which are crucial for accurate identification. This tool is especially useful for distinguishing between edible and toxic species.

2. Pocket Knife

A compact, foldable knife is a versatile tool for trimming plants, cutting roots, or peeling bark. Ensure your knife is sharp and clean to avoid unnecessary damage to plants.

3. A Walking Stick

A sturdy walking stick serves multiple purposes. It can help you navigate uneven terrain, probe dense undergrowth, or dislodge fruit from higher branches. Some foragers even customize their walking sticks with a hooked end for reaching into trees.

4. Water Bottle and Snacks

Foraging can be surprisingly physical, and staying hydrated is essential. Carry a refillable water bottle and a small snack to keep your energy levels up during extended trips.

5. Smartphone or GPS Device

While not essential, a smartphone with GPS capabilities can help you map foraging locations and avoid getting lost in unfamiliar areas. Many foragers also use their phones to take photos for later identification or documentation.

Maintaining and Caring for Your Tools

Your tools are an investment, and proper maintenance ensures they last for years. Regular cleaning, sharpening, and storage are key to keeping them in good condition.

- **Cleaning:** After each use, clean your tools to remove dirt,

sap, and plant residue. Use warm, soapy water for most tools and a disinfectant for items that come into contact with potentially contaminated plants.
- **Sharpening:** Keep blades sharp to ensure clean cuts and minimize damage to plants. Use a sharpening stone or tool specifically designed for pruners and knives.
- **Storage:** Store tools in a dry, cool place to prevent rust or degradation. Consider using a tool roll or designated container to keep everything organized.

Customizing Your Kit

Every forager's needs are different, and your tool kit should reflect your unique preferences and environment. As you gain experience, you'll develop a sense of which tools are indispensable and which can be left at home. For instance, urban foragers focusing on leafy greens might prioritize scissors and cloth bags, while those seeking berries or nuts might rely more on rigid containers and gloves.

Building Confidence with the Right Tools

Having the right tools isn't just about practicality; it's also about building confidence. Equipped with the appropriate gear, you'll feel more prepared to tackle the challenges of urban foraging, from identifying plants to harvesting them safely and efficiently. Over time, this confidence will translate into a deeper appreciation for the practice, encouraging you to explore new areas and expand your knowledge.

This chapter highlights the importance of preparation and the tools that make urban foraging a safe, enjoyable, and enriching experience. As you assemble your kit and familiarize yourself with its components, you'll be well-equipped to navigate the exciting world of urban foraging with skill and confidence.

Chapter 3: Understanding Urban Ecosystems

Urban ecosystems are a dynamic blend of natural and human-made environments. They are living, breathing networks where biodiversity interacts with urban infrastructure, shaping and reshaping the ways in which life flourishes amidst concrete and steel. To truly master the art of urban foraging, it is essential to understand these ecosystems—their components, challenges, and opportunities. This chapter delves into the complexities of urban ecosystems, offering insights into how they function and providing a roadmap for engaging with them responsibly and effectively.

---

1. What Defines an Urban Ecosystem?

Urban ecosystems encompass all living organisms (plants, animals, fungi, and microorganisms) and their physical environments within city settings. These environments include parks, gardens, rivers, abandoned lots, green rooftops, and even the cracks in sidewalks where hardy weeds emerge.

1.1 Key Features of Urban Ecosystems

- **Fragmentation:** Urban areas are highly fragmented, with

patches of green space interspersed among buildings and roads. This fragmentation affects biodiversity and the movement of species.
- **Anthropogenic Influence:** Human activity dominates urban ecosystems, shaping everything from soil composition to species distribution.
- **Novel Habitats:** Urban areas create unique habitats, such as building walls, gutters, and industrial zones, where organisms adapt to survive.
- **Biodiversity Hotspots:** While cities may seem devoid of nature, they often host surprising levels of biodiversity due to their varied microclimates and ecological niches.

1.2 The Importance of Urban Ecosystems

- **Ecosystem Services:** Urban ecosystems provide crucial services such as air purification, carbon sequestration, temperature regulation, and water filtration.
- **Food and Resources:** These ecosystems support wild edible plants, medicinal herbs, and materials for crafting.
- **Mental and Physical Well-being:** Access to green spaces improves mental health, encourages physical activity, and fosters a sense of community.

2. Components of Urban Ecosystems

Urban ecosystems are composed of both biotic (living) and abiotic (non-living) elements that interact in complex ways. Understanding these components can help foragers identify areas rich in resources and ensure sustainable practices.

2.1 Biotic Components

- **Flora (Plants):**
    - Wild edibles like dandelions, plantains, and chickweed thrive in urban environments.
    - Invasive species, such as Japanese knotweed and garlic mustard, often dominate disturbed areas.
    - Native plants play a crucial role in supporting local biodiversity.
- **Fauna (Animals):**
    - Pollinators like bees, butterflies, and beetles are essential for plant reproduction.
    - Birds and small mammals contribute to seed dispersal and pest control.
    - Predators like hawks and urban foxes help maintain ecological balance.
- **Fungi and Microorganisms:**
    - Fungi decompose organic matter, recycling

nutrients into the soil.
- Soil microorganisms support plant growth and contribute to nutrient cycles.

2.2 Abiotic Components

- **Soil:**
  - Urban soils are often compacted and contaminated but can still support a wide range of plant species.
  - Soil quality varies widely depending on location and history.
- **Water:**
  - Rivers, ponds, and stormwater systems are critical water sources for urban ecosystems.
  - Water availability and quality impact plant and animal life.
- **Climate:**
  - Cities experience unique climate phenomena, such as the urban heat island effect, which influences plant growth and species distribution.

3. Challenges Facing Urban Ecosystems

Urban ecosystems face numerous challenges, many of which stem from human activity. Recognizing these challenges is key to understanding the limitations and opportunities of foraging in cities.

3.1 Habitat Loss and Fragmentation

- **Development Pressure:** Expanding urban areas often lead to the destruction of natural habitats.
- **Connectivity Issues:** Fragmented green spaces make it difficult for wildlife to move and reproduce.

3.2 Pollution

- **Soil Contamination:** Heavy metals, pesticides, and industrial waste can accumulate in urban soils, posing risks to plant and human health.
- **Air Pollution:** Particulates from vehicles and industry can settle on plants, affecting their quality and safety.
- **Water Contamination:** Runoff from roads and industrial areas can pollute urban water bodies.

3.3 Invasive Species

- Non-native plants and animals can outcompete native species, reducing biodiversity and altering ecosystems.
- Some invasive species, like knotweed, are edible and can be harvested sustainably to mitigate their spread.

3.4 Climate Change

- Rising temperatures and changing rainfall patterns affect the growth cycles of plants and the behavior of animals.
- Extreme weather events, such as heatwaves and flooding, strain urban ecosystems.

---

4. Opportunities in Urban Ecosystems

Despite these challenges, urban ecosystems offer numerous opportunities for foragers, conservationists, and community members to engage with and enhance their environments.

4.1 Discovering Abundance

- **Edible Plants:** Hardy species like purslane, lamb's quarters, and nettles thrive in urban settings.
- **Medicinal Plants:** Urban areas host a variety of medicinal

herbs, including yarrow and elderberry.
- **Crafting Materials:** Willow branches, pinecones, and acorns are often found in parks and greenways.

4.2 Creating Green Corridors

- Planting native species along roadsides, riverbanks, and abandoned lots can connect fragmented habitats and support biodiversity.
- Green corridors benefit pollinators, birds, and other wildlife while providing foraging opportunities.

4.3 Leveraging Community Involvement

- Community gardens and urban farming initiatives can incorporate wild plants into their designs, increasing food security and biodiversity.
- Foraging groups and workshops promote awareness and sustainable practices.

---

5. Tools for Understanding and Navigating Urban Ecosystems

5.1 Observation Skills

- Pay attention to patterns in plant growth and animal behavior.
- Note changes in vegetation throughout the seasons to identify foraging opportunities.

5.2 Mapping Resources

- Use tools like Google Maps or apps like iNaturalist to document foraging sites and track plant species.
- Create a personal foraging map to plan sustainable harvests and revisit productive areas.

5.3 Testing Soil and Water Quality

- Home testing kits can help determine levels of contaminants like lead or pesticides.
- Avoid foraging in areas with visibly poor soil or polluted water sources.

5.4 Building Knowledge

- Invest in field guides specific to your region for accurate plant identification.
- Join local foraging or conservation groups to learn from experienced individuals.

6. The Role of Foragers in Urban Ecosystems

Urban foragers play a unique role in promoting sustainability, conservation, and community engagement. By interacting thoughtfully with these ecosystems, foragers can contribute to their health and resilience.

6.1 Advocates for Biodiversity

- Foragers can help raise awareness about the importance of native plants and the threats posed by invasive species.
- Participating in citizen science initiatives, such as documenting plant and animal species, contributes valuable data for conservation efforts.

6.2 Promoters of Sustainability

- Sustainable foraging practices ensure that urban ecosystems remain productive for future generations.
- Harvesting invasive plants, such as garlic mustard, can reduce their impact on native species.

6.3 Educators and Community Builders

- Sharing knowledge about urban ecosystems fosters a greater sense of connection and stewardship within

communities.
- Hosting workshops or guided walks can inspire others to engage with their local environments.

Understanding urban ecosystems is fundamental to becoming a skilled and responsible urban forager. By recognizing the intricate relationships between plants, animals, and human activity, foragers can navigate these landscapes with respect and confidence, unlocking the hidden abundance of cities.

Chapter 4: Top Wild Edibles Found in Cities

Urban landscapes, while dominated by concrete and steel, are surprisingly abundant with edible plants, many of which are overlooked or dismissed as weeds. These wild edibles, resilient and adaptable, thrive in parks, vacant lots, gardens, and even cracks in sidewalks. By learning to identify and utilize these plants, urban foragers can unlock a treasure trove of free, nutrient-rich food right at their doorstep.

In this chapter, we will explore some of the most common and versatile wild edibles found in cities. Each plant will be introduced with its defining characteristics, preferred habitat, nutritional benefits, and potential uses. Whether you're a beginner or an experienced forager, this guide will equip you with the knowledge to safely and confidently harvest nature's urban bounty.

---

1. Dandelion (Taraxacum officinale)

Description:

Dandelions are perhaps the most iconic urban edible, recognized by their bright yellow flowers and deeply toothed leaves. The plant's milky sap and fluffy seed heads further distinguish it from lookalikes.

Habitat:

Found almost everywhere, dandelions thrive in lawns, parks, roadside verges, and even sidewalk cracks. They prefer sunny locations and are incredibly resilient.

Edible Parts:

- **Leaves:** Best harvested young, dandelion leaves are slightly bitter and make excellent additions to salads, sautés, or pesto.
- **Flowers:** Use fresh or dried flowers in teas, syrups, or even homemade wine.
- **Roots:** Roast the roots to create a caffeine-free coffee substitute.

Nutritional Benefits:

Dandelions are rich in vitamins A, C, and K, as well as minerals like potassium and calcium. They also contain antioxidants and have diuretic properties.

2. Wild Garlic (Allium ursinum)

Description:

Wild garlic is easily identified by its strong garlicky aroma, broad green leaves, and delicate white flowers. It grows in clusters and is often mistaken for toxic lookalikes like lily of the valley, so careful identification is crucial.

Habitat:

Look for wild garlic in shaded areas such as urban woodlands, parks, and riverbanks.

Edible Parts:

- **Leaves:** Use raw in salads, blended into pesto, or as a garnish.
- **Flowers:** Sprinkle on dishes for a decorative and flavorful touch.
- **Bulbs:** Though less common in urban foraging, the bulbs can be used like regular garlic.

Nutritional Benefits:

Wild garlic is high in vitamins A and C, sulfur compounds, and antioxidants. It also has antimicrobial and heart-protective properties.

---

3. Chickweed (Stellaria media)

Description:

This low-growing plant features small, star-shaped white flowers and smooth, succulent leaves. It has a delicate, mild flavor.

Habitat:

Chickweed thrives in moist, shaded areas such as garden beds, parks, and urban waste spaces.

Edible Parts:

- **Leaves and Stems:** Add to salads, smoothies, or sautés for a fresh, green flavor.
- **Flowers:** Edible and visually appealing as garnishes.

Nutritional Benefits:

Chickweed is packed with vitamins C and A, iron, and magnesium. It is also known for its anti-inflammatory and cooling properties.

---

4. Purslane (Portulaca oleracea)

Description:

Purslane is a succulent with fleshy, reddish stems and small, oval-shaped leaves. It has a tangy, slightly lemony taste and grows in sprawling mats.

Habitat:

Often found in sunny, disturbed soils such as garden beds, driveways, and sidewalks.

Edible Parts:

- **Leaves and Stems:** Eat raw in salads or sauté them as a side dish.
- **Seeds:** Use as a nutritious topping for baked goods or smoothies.

Nutritional Benefits:

Purslane is a nutritional powerhouse, containing high levels of omega-3 fatty acids, vitamin C, and beta-carotene. It's also a good source of magnesium and potassium.

---

5. Plantain (Plantago spp.)

Description:

Plantains are characterized by their broad, ribbed leaves and tall flower spikes. Not to be confused with the banana-like fruit, plantain is a common urban weed with medicinal uses.

Habitat:

Grows in compacted soils, such as lawns, driveways, and pathways.

Edible Parts:

- **Leaves:** Young leaves can be eaten raw or cooked like spinach.
- **Seeds:** Harvest the seeds for a high-fiber addition to baked goods.

Nutritional Benefits:

Plantain leaves are rich in vitamins A, C, and K, as well as calcium and iron. They also have anti-inflammatory properties.

---

6. Wood Sorrel (Oxalis spp.)

Description:

Wood sorrel has clover-like leaves and small, yellow flowers. It has a pleasantly sour taste due to its oxalic acid content.

Habitat:

Common in lawns, gardens, and shaded urban areas.

Edible Parts:

- **Leaves, Flowers, and Stems:** Use as a tangy garnish or in soups and salads.

Nutritional Benefits:

Wood sorrel provides vitamin C and antioxidants. However, it should be consumed in moderation due to its oxalic acid content.

7. Lamb's Quarters (Chenopodium album)

Description:

Also known as wild spinach, lamb's quarters has triangular, gray-green leaves with a powdery coating on the underside.

Habitat:

Thrives in disturbed soils, such as gardens, alleys, and vacant lots.

Edible Parts:

- **Leaves:** Cook like spinach or use raw in salads.
- **Seeds:** Use ground seeds as a flour substitute.

Nutritional Benefits:

Lamb's quarters is rich in protein, vitamins A and C, calcium, and iron. It's an excellent substitute for spinach in any recipe.

8. Mulberries (Morus spp.)

Description:

Mulberry trees produce small, blackberry-like fruits that range in color from red to black. Their heart-shaped leaves are also edible when cooked.

Habitat:

Often found in parks, backyards, and along sidewalks.

Edible Parts:

- **Fruits:** Eat fresh, or use in jams, desserts, and smoothies.
- **Leaves:** Use young leaves in soups or teas.

Nutritional Benefits:

Mulberries are high in vitamin C, iron, and antioxidants. They're also a natural source of resveratrol, a compound linked to heart health.

9. Stinging Nettle (Urtica dioica)

Description:

Stinging nettles are known for their jagged leaves and tiny stinging hairs. Proper preparation neutralizes the sting and reveals their rich flavor.

Habitat:

Found in shaded, moist areas such as parks, riverbanks, and garden edges.

Edible Parts:

- **Leaves and Stems:** Cook thoroughly to use in soups, sautés, or teas.

Nutritional Benefits:

Nettles are exceptionally nutrient-dense, offering high levels of vitamins A, C, and K, iron, calcium, and protein.

10. Elderflower and Elderberries (Sambucus spp.)

Description:

Elder plants feature clusters of white flowers and small, dark purple berries. The flowers have a sweet aroma, while the berries are tart and slightly bitter.

Habitat:

Found in urban parks, gardens, and along fences.

Edible Parts:

- **Flowers:** Use to make cordials, syrups, or teas.
- **Berries:** Cook into jams, syrups, or pies. Avoid eating raw, as they can cause stomach upset.

Nutritional Benefits:

Elderflowers and elderberries are rich in antioxidants and vitamins, particularly vitamin C. They are also used traditionally for immune support.

Chapter 5: Seasonal Foraging: What to Look For and When

Foraging, by its very nature, is deeply tied to the rhythms of the seasons. Plants follow cycles of growth, flowering, and fruiting that are dictated by the ebb and flow of the seasons. Understanding these cycles is essential for successful and sustainable foraging. Seasonal foraging not only ensures that you harvest plants at their peak of flavor and nutrition but also deepens your connection to nature's rhythms. Each season brings its own unique bounty, and learning what to look for and when to harvest can transform your foraging experience.

In this chapter, we will explore the art of seasonal foraging in detail, breaking down the specific plants, fruits, and fungi to seek out in each season. Along the way, we'll share tips for identifying seasonal opportunities, managing your foraging schedule, and making the most of nature's calendar.

Spring: A Time of Renewal

Spring is the season of rebirth, and it's one of the most exciting times for foragers. As the ground thaws and temperatures rise, a host of tender greens, shoots, and early blossoms emerge.

These plants are often at their most flavorful and nutrient-rich during this period.

1. Dandelions

- **What to Look For:** Young, tender leaves before the plant flowers. The bright yellow flowers can also be harvested for teas and syrups.
- **Best Time to Harvest:** Early to mid-spring.
- **Uses:** Raw in salads, sautéed, or made into wine or tea.

2. Wild Garlic

- **What to Look For:** Broad, green leaves and small white flowers. The distinctive garlic scent is a key identifier.
- **Best Time to Harvest:** Early spring, before the flowers fully bloom.
- **Uses:** Pestos, soups, and as a seasoning.

3. Nettles

- **What to Look For:** Bright green, young shoots. Always wear gloves to avoid the sting.
- **Best Time to Harvest:** Early spring when shoots are under 30 cm tall.
- **Uses:** Soups, sautés, or dried for tea.

4. Chickweed

- **What to Look For:** Fresh, succulent leaves and small white flowers. Chickweed grows rapidly in cool weather.
- **Best Time to Harvest:** Throughout spring.
- **Uses:** Raw in salads or as a mild green in sautés.

5. Wood Sorrel

- **What to Look For:** Clover-like leaves and small yellow or pink flowers. The tangy, lemony flavor is unmistakable.
- **Best Time to Harvest:** Late spring.
- **Uses:** Salads, garnishes, or refreshing drinks.

Summer: Abundance and Variety

Summer is the season of abundance, offering a diverse range of plants, fruits, and edible flowers. This is also the time when berries and tree fruits come into their own, adding sweetness to your foraging haul.

1. Purslane

- **What to Look For:** Fleshy, succulent stems with small, oval-shaped leaves. Purslane grows in sunny, disturbed areas.
- **Best Time to Harvest:** Midsummer to late summer.
- **Uses:** Salads, sautés, or blended into smoothies.

2. Lamb's Quarters

- **What to Look For:** Powdery, triangular leaves and upright growth. These are often found in gardens and fields.
- **Best Time to Harvest:** Early to midsummer.
- **Uses:** Cook like spinach or eat raw in salads.

3. Elderflowers

- **What to Look For:** Clusters of fragrant white flowers on elder trees. Avoid flowers near roads or sprayed areas.
- **Best Time to Harvest:** Early summer.
- **Uses:** Syrups, cordials, or desserts.

4. Blackberries

- **What to Look For:** Ripe, juicy berries that pull easily from the vine. Avoid underripe, red ones.
- **Best Time to Harvest:** Late summer.
- **Uses:** Pies, jams, or fresh eating.

5. Wild Herbs (e.g., Mint, Thyme)

- **What to Look For:** Vibrant, aromatic leaves. Many wild herbs flourish in summer.
- **Best Time to Harvest:** Throughout summer.
- **Uses:** Teas, marinades, or seasoning blends.

Autumn: Harvest Season

Autumn is the pinnacle of foraging, as many plants reach maturity and bear fruit. This season is particularly known for nuts, fungi, and hearty greens.

1. Acorns

- **What to Look For:** Fully mature, brown acorns that have fallen from the tree. Discard any with holes or black spots.
- **Best Time to Harvest:** Mid to late autumn.
- **Uses:** Leach tannins out of acorns to make flour or roast them for snacks.

2. Mushrooms (e.g., Chanterelles, Puffballs)

- **What to Look For:** Fresh, firm specimens in wooded areas. Mushroom foraging requires precise identification.
- **Best Time to Harvest:** Early to late autumn, depending on species.
- **Uses:** Soups, sautés, or drying for storage.

3. Rosehips

- **What to Look For:** Bright red or orange fruits left after roses have bloomed. Choose firm, unwrinkled ones.
- **Best Time to Harvest:** Late autumn, after the first frost.
- **Uses:** Teas, syrups, or jams.

4. Walnuts and Hazelnuts

- **What to Look For:** Nuts with intact shells. Harvest directly from the ground or shake branches to release them.
- **Best Time to Harvest:** Mid-autumn.
- **Uses:** Snacking, baking, or making nut butter.

5. Apples and Crabapples

- **What to Look For:** Firm, ripe fruits with bright coloring. Avoid bruised or wormy specimens.
- **Best Time to Harvest:** Early to mid-autumn.
- **Uses:** Pies, sauces, or cider.

Winter: Hidden Treasures

While winter might seem like a barren time for foraging, a few hardy plants and stored resources make it a worthwhile season for dedicated foragers.

1. Pine Needles

- **What to Look For:** Fresh, green needles from non-toxic pine species. Avoid brown or dry needles.
- **Best Time to Harvest:** Throughout winter.
- **Uses:** Tea rich in vitamin C or as a flavoring agent.

2. Wintercress

- **What to Look For:** Low-growing rosettes of dark green leaves. Wintercress is one of the few greens that thrives in the cold.
- **Best Time to Harvest:** Early to mid-winter.
- **Uses:** Salads, sautés, or as a spicy garnish.

3. Frozen Berries

- **What to Look For:** Leftover berries on shrubs, preserved naturally by frost. Look for species like cranberries or rosehips.
- **Best Time to Harvest:** Early winter.
- **Uses:** Teas, jams, or sauces.

4. Roots (e.g., Burdock, Dandelion)

- **What to Look For:** Dig up roots from established plants. Soil is softer in winter, making roots easier to extract.
- **Best Time to Harvest:** Throughout winter.
- **Uses:** Roasted or dried for teas and infusions.

Tips for Successful Seasonal Foraging

1. **Know Your Local Climate:** Seasonal availability varies by region. Research local flora to align your foraging calendar with the environment.
2. **Plan Ahead:** Some plants and fruits have short harvest windows. Mark your calendar to avoid missing these prime times.
3. **Rotate Locations:** Avoid overharvesting in a single spot by alternating your foraging areas each season.

4. **Preserve Your Harvest:** Learn preservation techniques such as drying, fermenting, and freezing to enjoy seasonal finds year-round.
5. **Track Your Finds:** Keep a foraging journal to record what you find, when, and where. Over time, this will help you anticipate seasonal harvests.

By understanding the seasonal patterns of wild edibles, you can maximize your foraging efforts while ensuring sustainability. Each season brings its own unique opportunities, and with a little knowledge and preparation, you can enjoy a year-round connection to the natural world.

Chapter 6: Avoiding Danger: Poisonous Lookalikes and

Contaminated Areas

Foraging can be a deeply rewarding experience, offering a connection to nature, a sense of accomplishment, and access to fresh, nutrient-dense foods. However, it also comes with its risks. Among the most critical challenges for foragers are poisonous plant lookalikes and the potential contamination of urban foraging sites. Safety must always come first when venturing into the wild or urban green spaces to collect edible plants, fungi, or fruits.

In this chapter, we will explore how to identify and avoid toxic plants that resemble edible ones, how to assess the safety of foraging locations, and how to minimize the risks associated with consuming wild edibles. By the end, you will have a solid understanding of how to protect yourself while enjoying the full benefits of foraging.

---

1. Poisonous Lookalikes: A Threat to Safety

One of the most significant risks for foragers is the presence of poisonous plants that closely resemble edible species. Even experienced foragers must remain vigilant, as small identification errors can lead to serious consequences, including severe illness or death.

The Importance of Plant Identification

Accurate plant identification is non-negotiable in foraging. Invest in high-quality field guides, attend foraging workshops, and practice your identification skills regularly. Always cross-reference plants using multiple sources before consuming them, and when in doubt, leave it out.

Common Poisonous Lookalikes

Below are some examples of common edible plants and their toxic counterparts to watch for:

Wild Garlic (Allium ursinum) vs. Lily of the Valley (Convallaria majalis)

- **Wild Garlic:** Broad green leaves, strong garlic scent, and small white flowers.
- **Lily of the Valley:** Similar leaf shape but lacks the garlic scent. Contains toxic compounds that can cause nausea, vomiting, and heart irregularities.
- **Tip:** Crush a leaf between your fingers to check for the characteristic garlic aroma.

Queen Anne's Lace (Daucus carota) vs. Poison Hemlock (Conium

maculatum)

- **Queen Anne's Lace:** Lacy white flower clusters, hairy stems, and a carrot-like smell.
- **Poison Hemlock:** Smooth stems with purple blotches, no hair, and an unpleasant odor. All parts are highly toxic.
- **Tip:** Avoid any plant that resembles Queen Anne's Lace but lacks a hairy stem or smells unpleasant.

Edible Berries vs. Poisonous Berries

- **Blackberries and Raspberries:** Aggregate berries with a sweet taste.
- **Deadly Nightshade (Atropa belladonna):** Glossy black or dark purple berries, often solitary, growing from toxic plants.
- **Tip:** Stick to aggregate berries that grow in clusters. Avoid solitary berries unless you are certain of their identity.

Elderberries (Sambucus nigra) vs. Pokeberries (Phytolacca americana)

- **Elderberries:** Small, dark purple or black berries growing in clusters, edible only when cooked.
- **Pokeberries:** Bright purple berries on magenta stems. Toxic to humans and animals.
- **Tip:** Avoid any plant with vibrant magenta stems and

brightly colored berries.

Wild Parsnip (Pastinaca sativa) vs. Giant Hogweed (Heracleum mantegazzianum)

- **Wild Parsnip:** Smaller leaves and flowers, with a less aggressive sap.
- **Giant Hogweed:** Huge leaves and umbrella-shaped flower clusters. Its sap causes severe burns when exposed to sunlight.
- **Tip:** Wear gloves and protective clothing when handling any member of the carrot family (Apiaceae).

---

2. Recognizing Toxic Fungi

Fungi present an even greater identification challenge than plants. Edible mushrooms often have deadly doppelgängers, making it essential to proceed with caution when foraging for fungi.

Golden Rules for Mushroom Safety

1. Never eat a mushroom unless you are 100% certain of its identity.
2. Use multiple sources to confirm identification, including

field guides, mushroom experts, and apps.
3. Learn the defining features of common toxic mushrooms.

Toxic Mushroom Lookalikes

Morels (Morchella spp.) vs. False Morels (Gyromitra spp.)

- **Morels:** Honeycomb-like caps with hollow stems.
- **False Morels:** Irregular, brain-like caps with solid or chambered stems. Contains gyromitrin, a toxic compound.
- **Tip:** Cut the mushroom in half to confirm its hollow stem.

Chanterelles (Cantharellus spp.) vs. Jack-O'-Lanterns (Omphalotus spp.)

- **Chanterelles:** Funnel-shaped, with forked gills and a fruity aroma.
- **Jack-O'-Lanterns:** Bright orange, with true gills that run down the stem. Bioluminescent in the dark.
- **Tip:** Examine the gill structure closely and check for a fruity scent.

Parasol Mushrooms (Macrolepiota procera) vs. Green-Spored Parasol

(Chlorophyllum molybdites)

- **Parasol Mushrooms:** Large caps with a snakeskin-like pattern on the stem and white spores.
- **Green-Spored Parasol:** Similar appearance but with greenish spores. Causes severe gastrointestinal distress.
- **Tip:** Perform a spore print test to confirm the color.

3. Identifying Contaminated Foraging Areas

Urban foraging introduces unique risks, as plants in cities are more likely to be exposed to contaminants. These can include heavy metals, pesticides, herbicides, and pollutants from traffic or industry.

Signs of Contaminated Areas

1. Proximity to Roads

- Plants near busy roads may absorb pollutants such as lead, cadmium, and hydrocarbons.
- **Tip:** Avoid foraging within 50 feet of heavy traffic areas.

2. Industrial Sites

- Factories, railroads, and landfills may leach chemicals

into the soil and water.
- **Tip:** Research the history of the site before foraging.

3. Treated Lawns and Parks

- Herbicides and pesticides are commonly used in public parks and residential lawns.
- **Tip:** Look for signs indicating recent chemical applications, such as warning markers.

4. Urban Water Sources

- Rivers, streams, and ponds in urban areas may be contaminated with runoff or sewage.
- **Tip:** Test water sources or avoid aquatic plants from questionable areas.

Tools for Assessing Soil and Water Safety

1. **pH Test Kits:** Check for abnormal soil pH levels.
2. **Heavy Metal Test Kits:** Detect the presence of lead, cadmium, and arsenic.
3. **Water Testing Kits:** Evaluate water sources for contaminants like E. coli or heavy metals.

4. Minimizing Risks in Foraging

Once you've identified a safe foraging location and ruled out poisonous lookalikes, there are additional precautions you can take to ensure your harvest is safe to consume.

Best Practices for Cleaning Foraged Foods

1. **Wash Thoroughly:** Rinse plants under running water to remove dirt, insects, and surface contaminants.
2. **Soak in Salt Water:** For leafy greens and herbs, a saltwater soak can help remove hidden pests.
3. **Peel or Trim:** Remove the outer layers of roots, stems, or fruits to eliminate potential contaminants.
4. **Cook When in Doubt:** Heat can neutralize some toxins and reduce microbial risks. For example, elderberries must be cooked to remove their toxic compounds.

Building a Foraging Safety Kit

- **Field Guide:** A comprehensive guide with photos and detailed descriptions.
- **Magnifying Glass:** For examining plant and mushroom details.
- **Gloves:** To protect your hands from irritants or toxic sap.

- **Notebook or App:** To document your finds and revisit safe locations.
- **Test Kits:** For soil and water quality assessments.

5. Educating Yourself and Others

Foraging safety is a skill that improves with knowledge and practice. Share your experiences with others, attend workshops, and engage with the foraging community to deepen your understanding of plants and their environments.

Resources for Continued Learning

1. **Books:** Expand your library with region-specific foraging books.
2. **Foraging Groups:** Join local clubs or online forums to share tips and experiences.
3. **Workshops and Walks:** Participate in guided foraging walks led by experts.

By understanding and addressing the risks of poisonous lookalikes and contaminated areas, you can enjoy the full benefits of foraging while staying safe.

Chapter 7: Harvesting and Storing Your Finds

Harvesting and storing wild edibles is both an art and a science. Foraging successfully isn't just about identifying and collecting plants, fruits, or fungi; it's also about knowing when and how to harvest them to ensure the best flavor, nutrition, and sustainability. Proper storage methods are equally critical, allowing you to make the most of your finds, reduce waste, and enjoy the fruits of your labor well beyond the foraging season.

In this chapter, we'll explore the principles of ethical harvesting, techniques for gathering various types of wild edibles, and best practices for preserving your foraged bounty. From drying and freezing to fermenting and pickling, this comprehensive guide will prepare you to harvest and store your finds like a seasoned forager.

1. Principles of Ethical Harvesting

Foraging is inherently a practice rooted in respect for nature. Ethical harvesting ensures that you're not only taking what you need but also leaving enough for plants to regenerate and for wildlife to thrive.

1.1 Take Only What You Need

- **Golden Rule:** Harvest no more than 10% of a plant's available bounty in a given area. This ensures that the plant can continue to grow and reproduce.
- **Wildlife Considerations:** Remember that animals and insects rely on the same resources. Leave enough behind to support the ecosystem.

1.2 Avoid Overharvesting

- Focus on abundant and invasive species rather than rare or endangered ones.
- Familiarize yourself with local laws and protected plants in your area to avoid unintentional harm.

1.3 Minimize Damage

- Use sharp tools like scissors, pruners, or knives to make clean cuts rather than tearing plants.
- Avoid trampling surrounding vegetation or disturbing soil unnecessarily.

1.4 Be Mindful of Seasons

- Harvest plants at their peak but avoid collecting too early or late in their life cycle.

- For perennial plants, ensure you're not taking more than the plant can recover from before the next growing season.

---

2. Timing Your Harvest

Knowing when to harvest is crucial for both flavor and nutrition. Different plants and fungi have specific times when they're at their best.

2.1 Morning Harvests

- Many plants are most flavorful and hydrated in the early morning after dew has settled but before the sun dries them out.
- Examples: Leafy greens like dandelion, chickweed, and lamb's quarters.

2.2 Seasonal Awareness

- **Spring:** Focus on tender greens, wild garlic, and early shoots.
- **Summer:** Collect fruits, berries, and flowering herbs.
- **Autumn:** Harvest roots, nuts, and fungi.

- **Winter:** Seek hardy plants like wintercress and evergreen herbs.

2.3 Observing Plant Health

- Avoid harvesting from stressed, diseased, or pest-damaged plants.
- Look for vibrant colors, firm textures, and healthy leaves.

---

3. Techniques for Harvesting Different Types of Wild Edibles

3.1 Leafy Greens and Herbs

- Use sharp scissors or pruners to snip leaves cleanly, leaving the plant base intact.
- Avoid overharvesting from a single plant; take only a few leaves per stem.

3.2 Fruits and Berries

- Gently twist or pull ripe fruits to avoid damaging branches.
- Use a basket or container to prevent crushing delicate fruits like mulberries or raspberries.

- Shake bushes gently to collect fallen fruits, a traditional technique for elderberries.

3.3 Roots and Tubers

- Dig carefully with a trowel or foraging stick to minimize soil disruption.
- Refill the hole to leave the ecosystem undisturbed.
- Example: Harvest dandelion or burdock roots in late autumn for their highest nutrient content.

3.4 Nuts and Seeds

- Collect nuts directly from the ground, ensuring they're intact and free of pests.
- Harvest seeds like wild fennel by clipping mature flower heads and shaking them into a bag.

3.5 Mushrooms

- Use a knife to cut mushrooms at the base, leaving the mycelium undisturbed.
- Carry fungi in a breathable basket to prevent them from becoming slimy.
- Avoid waterlogged or decaying specimens.

4. Best Practices for Cleaning Your Foraged Finds

Cleaning your foraged edibles is an essential step to remove dirt, insects, and potential contaminants.

4.1 General Cleaning Tips

- **Rinse Immediately:** Wash greens, fruits, and herbs under cold running water soon after harvesting.
- **Saltwater Soak:** Soak greens in a solution of saltwater to dislodge insects.
- **Brush Mushrooms:** Use a soft brush to clean mushrooms instead of washing, as water can affect their texture.

4.2 Special Considerations for Urban Foraging

- Avoid collecting plants near heavy traffic or industrial sites due to potential contamination.
- Test soil or water quality if you're unsure about the safety of your foraging location.

---

5. Storing Your Finds

Proper storage techniques help preserve the flavor, texture, and nutritional value of your foraged edibles. Different types of foods require different methods.

5.1 Refrigeration

- **Leafy Greens:** Wrap in a damp cloth or place in a container with a paper towel to maintain freshness.
- **Berries:** Store unwashed in a single layer to prevent mold.
- **Herbs:** Keep stems in a jar of water, covered loosely with a plastic bag.

5.2 Freezing

- **Blanching:** Briefly boil greens like nettles or dandelion leaves before freezing to retain color and nutrients.
- **Fruits and Berries:** Freeze on a tray before transferring to bags to prevent clumping.
- **Mushrooms:** Sauté before freezing to maintain texture.

5.3 Drying

- **Herbs:** Hang bundles upside-down in a warm, dark, well-ventilated area.
- **Fruits:** Use a dehydrator or oven set to low heat to dry apple slices, mulberries, or rosehips.
- **Mushrooms:** Air-dry or use a dehydrator, ensuring they're fully dried to prevent mold.

5.4 Pickling and Fermenting

- **Pickling:** Preserve greens, roots, or mushrooms in vinegar-based solutions with spices for flavor.
- **Fermenting:** Create probiotic-rich foods like kimchi or sauerkraut using wild greens.

5.5 Making Infusions

- **Oils:** Infuse herbs like wild garlic or rosemary into olive oil for long-term storage.
- **Alcohol:** Preserve fruits like elderberries in vodka or brandy to make tinctures or cordials.

---

6. Extending Shelf Life and Reducing Waste

6.1 Creative Uses for Surplus Finds

- Make jams, jellies, or syrups from excess berries.
- Turn herbs into pestos or dried spice blends.
- Blend greens into smoothies or freeze them in cubes for later use.

6.2 Rotating Stock

- Use older stored items first to prevent spoilage.
- Label containers with harvest dates.

6.3 Sharing and Bartering

- Share surplus with friends, family, or community members.
- Barter excess foraged goods with other foragers or local farmers.

Mastering the art of harvesting and storing wild edibles is a critical step in your foraging journey. By following these techniques and tips, you can enjoy the flavors and benefits of your foraged finds year-round while maintaining a sustainable and respectful relationship with nature.

Chapter 8: Simple Recipes with Urban Foraged Ingredients

Foraging in urban environments offers not just the joy of discovery but also the opportunity to transform wild ingredients into delicious meals. Cooking with foraged foods connects us to the land in a unique way, infusing our meals with the essence of the seasons. In this chapter, we'll explore simple yet inspiring recipes that make the most of your urban foraged finds. These recipes are designed to be accessible, using basic kitchen tools and common pantry staples to elevate wild ingredients into flavorful dishes.

---

1. Foraged Green Pesto

A versatile and nutrient-packed sauce, this pesto is a perfect way to use wild greens like dandelion leaves, chickweed, or purslane. Use it as a pasta sauce, sandwich spread, or dip.

Ingredients:

- 2 cups foraged greens (dandelion leaves, chickweed, or a mix)
- 1/4 cup nuts or seeds (pine nuts, walnuts, or sunflower seeds)

- 1/4 cup grated Parmesan cheese (or nutritional yeast for a vegan version)
- 2 cloves garlic
- 1/2 cup olive oil
- Juice of 1 lemon
- Salt and pepper to taste

Instructions:

1. Wash and dry the greens thoroughly.
2. In a food processor, combine the greens, nuts or seeds, Parmesan cheese, and garlic. Pulse until roughly chopped.
3. Slowly add the olive oil while processing, until the mixture reaches your desired consistency.
4. Stir in lemon juice, then season with salt and pepper to taste.
5. Store in a sealed jar in the refrigerator for up to one week.

---

2. Wild Garlic Soup

This creamy, aromatic soup is a celebration of wild garlic, which adds a mellow garlicky flavor without overpowering the dish.

Ingredients:

- 2 cups wild garlic leaves, washed and chopped
- 1 medium onion, diced
- 2 medium potatoes, peeled and diced
- 4 cups vegetable broth
- 1/2 cup heavy cream (optional for a richer soup)
- 2 tbsp olive oil
- Salt and pepper to taste

Instructions:

1. Heat olive oil in a large pot over medium heat. Add the onion and sauté until translucent.
2. Add the potatoes and cook for another 5 minutes.
3. Pour in the vegetable broth and bring to a boil. Reduce heat and simmer until the potatoes are tender.
4. Stir in the wild garlic leaves and cook for 2-3 minutes.
5. Use an immersion blender to puree the soup until smooth.
6. Stir in heavy cream if using, and season with salt and pepper.
7. Serve hot, garnished with a drizzle of olive oil or a sprinkle of fresh wild garlic leaves.

3. Elderflower Cordial

This fragrant cordial is a refreshing summer treat. Mix it with sparkling water or use it as a base for cocktails.

Ingredients:

- 20 elderflower heads, shaken to remove insects
- 4 cups water
- 4 cups sugar
- Zest and juice of 2 lemons
- 1 tsp citric acid (optional, for preservation)

Instructions:

1. In a large pot, bring the water to a boil. Remove from heat and stir in the sugar until dissolved.
2. Add the elderflower heads, lemon zest, and lemon juice to the pot. Stir well.
3. Cover and let steep for 24 hours.
4. Strain the mixture through a fine sieve or muslin cloth into sterilized bottles.
5. Store in the refrigerator for up to a month or process in a water bath for longer shelf life.

4. Dandelion Fritter Cakes

These crispy fritters make a delightful appetizer or snack, showcasing the floral sweetness of dandelion blooms.

Ingredients:

- 1 cup dandelion flowers, washed and patted dry
- 1/2 cup all-purpose flour
- 1/2 cup milk or plant-based alternative
- 1 egg
- 1/4 tsp salt
- Oil for frying

Instructions:

1. In a bowl, whisk together the flour, milk, egg, and salt to create a smooth batter.
2. Heat oil in a frying pan over medium heat.
3. Dip each dandelion flower into the batter, ensuring it's fully coated.
4. Fry the flowers in batches until golden brown, about 2 minutes per side.
5. Remove and drain on paper towels. Serve warm with a drizzle of honey or a sprinkle of powdered sugar.

5. Purslane and Tomato Salad

This vibrant salad highlights the tangy flavor of purslane, paired with the sweetness of ripe tomatoes.

Ingredients:

- 2 cups purslane leaves, washed
- 2 medium tomatoes, diced
- 1 small cucumber, sliced
- 1/4 red onion, thinly sliced
- 2 tbsp olive oil
- 1 tbsp balsamic vinegar
- Salt and pepper to taste

Instructions:

1. In a large bowl, combine the purslane, tomatoes, cucumber, and red onion.
2. Drizzle with olive oil and balsamic vinegar.
3. Toss gently to combine, then season with salt and pepper.
4. Serve immediately as a side dish or light lunch.

6. Stinging Nettle Tea

A simple and soothing tea, stinging nettle is known for its earthy flavor and health benefits.

Ingredients:

- 1 cup fresh stinging nettle leaves (wear gloves while handling)
- 2 cups boiling water
- Honey or lemon to taste (optional)

Instructions:

1. Rinse the nettle leaves thoroughly.
2. Place the leaves in a teapot and pour over boiling water.
3. Let steep for 5-10 minutes.
4. Strain into a cup and sweeten with honey or lemon if desired.
5. Enjoy warm or chilled.

---

7. Mulberry Jam

Preserve the sweetness of summer with this easy mulberry jam recipe.

Ingredients:

- 4 cups fresh mulberries, washed and stems removed
- 2 cups sugar
- 2 tbsp lemon juice

Instructions:

1. In a large pot, combine the mulberries, sugar, and lemon juice.
2. Heat over medium heat, stirring frequently, until the sugar dissolves.
3. Bring to a boil and cook until the mixture thickens, about 20 minutes.
4. Test for doneness by placing a small amount on a chilled plate; it should gel slightly.
5. Pour the jam into sterilized jars and seal. Store in the refrigerator or process in a water bath for longer storage.

---

8. Acorn Flour Pancakes

Nutty and earthy, these pancakes are a fantastic use of foraged acorns.

Ingredients:

- 1 cup acorn flour (prepared by leaching tannins)
- 1 cup all-purpose flour
- 2 tbsp sugar
- 1 tbsp baking powder
- 1/2 tsp salt
- 1 egg
- 1 1/4 cups milk or plant-based alternative
- 2 tbsp melted butter or oil

Instructions:

1. In a large bowl, whisk together the dry ingredients.
2. In a separate bowl, beat the egg, milk, and melted butter.
3. Gradually add the wet ingredients to the dry, stirring until just combined.
4. Heat a griddle or frying pan over medium heat and lightly grease.
5. Pour 1/4 cup batter for each pancake and cook until bubbles form on the surface. Flip and cook until golden brown.
6. Serve with syrup, honey, or fresh berries.

This chapter transforms the foraged ingredients you've gathered into delicious dishes that celebrate their unique flavors and versatility. By incorporating these recipes into your cooking repertoire, you'll not only enjoy the fruits of your foraging but also deepen your connection to the natural world through the joy of sharing meals made from wild, urban ingredients.

Chapter 9: Building Community Through Urban Foraging

Urban foraging is often seen as a solitary activity, a quiet pursuit of nature's offerings amid the bustle of city life. However, foraging has the power to bring people together, fostering a sense of community and collective purpose. By sharing knowledge, experiences, and the fruits of the urban landscape, foragers can build strong connections that enhance both their practice and their relationships. In this chapter, we will explore the various ways urban foraging can create and strengthen communities, from organizing group foraging walks to engaging in community projects and sharing resources.

---

1. The Social Benefits of Urban Foraging

Foraging has an inherently social component. It invites collaboration, the exchange of knowledge, and shared experiences that deepen bonds between individuals and groups. By stepping into nature together, foragers create opportunities for connection and mutual support.

1.1 Knowledge Sharing

- **Intergenerational Learning:** Urban foraging offers a platform for the transfer of knowledge between generations. Elders

can share traditional wisdom about local plants, while younger participants bring fresh perspectives and technological tools like plant identification apps.
- **Skill Exchange:** Different foragers often specialize in unique areas, such as fungi identification, herbal medicine, or cooking with wild ingredients. Sharing these skills enriches the entire group.

1.2 Creating Shared Memories

- Group foraging experiences often become cherished memories. Whether it's the joy of discovering an abundant patch of wild garlic or the camaraderie of cooking a shared meal with foraged ingredients, these moments foster a sense of belonging.

1.3 Building Trust and Cooperation

- Foraging together encourages teamwork and mutual respect. Participants learn to share resources, navigate disagreements about harvesting practices, and support one another's safety and learning.

2. Organizing Group Foraging Walks

One of the simplest and most effective ways to build community through urban foraging is by organizing group foraging walks. These events can bring together people of all ages and skill levels, creating an inclusive space for learning and connection.

2.1 Planning a Foraging Walk

- **Choosing a Location:** Select a diverse and accessible area, such as a city park, urban woodland, or riverbank. Ensure the site is safe and legal for foraging.
- **Timing:** Schedule the walk during a peak foraging season, such as spring for wild greens or autumn for nuts and fungi.
- **Permits and Permissions:** Check local regulations to confirm that group foraging is allowed in your chosen location.

2.2 Leading the Walk

- **Preparation:** Research the area beforehand to identify key plants and ensure accurate knowledge.
- **Guidance:** Provide clear instructions on ethical harvesting, plant identification, and safety precautions.
- **Engagement:** Encourage participation by asking questions, inviting attendees to share their experiences,

and demonstrating how to harvest and use the plants.

2.3 Tips for a Successful Walk

- Bring visual aids, such as laminated plant identification cards or books.
- Provide small collection bags or baskets for participants.
- End the walk with a communal activity, such as preparing a simple dish with the collected ingredients or sharing a picnic.

3. Creating Foraging Networks

Foraging networks are communities of like-minded individuals who share resources, knowledge, and opportunities. These networks can be as informal as a group of friends or as structured as an organized club or online forum.

3.1 Starting a Local Foraging Club

- **Recruit Members:** Spread the word through social media, community boards, or local events. Emphasize inclusivity and welcome participants of all skill levels.
- **Set Goals:** Define the club's purpose, such as education,

conservation, or culinary exploration.
- **Organize Events:** Plan regular activities, such as foraging walks, workshops, or cooking demonstrations.
- **Stay Connected:** Use group messaging apps or online platforms to share updates, photos, and tips.

3.2 Online Foraging Communities

- **Social Media Groups:** Platforms like Facebook or Reddit host numerous foraging groups where members exchange advice, photos, and location tips.
- **Apps and Forums:** Tools like iNaturalist and Mushroom Observer allow foragers to connect, identify plants, and document findings collaboratively.

4. Collaborating on Community Projects

Urban foraging can inspire larger community initiatives that benefit both people and the environment. By working together, foragers can create impactful projects that promote sustainability, education, and access to natural resources.

4.1 Establishing Community Gardens

- **Foraging Integration:** Incorporate edible wild plants into the garden design to blend cultivated and foraged elements.
- **Workshops:** Host educational sessions on identifying and using wild plants in the garden.
- **Shared Harvests:** Encourage members to share their harvests, fostering a spirit of generosity and cooperation.

4.2 Organizing Foraging Workshops and Classes

- **Topics:** Offer workshops on plant identification, ethical foraging, or cooking with wild ingredients.
- **Guest Speakers:** Invite local experts, such as herbalists, chefs, or ecologists, to share their knowledge.
- **Youth Programs:** Engage younger generations by incorporating foraging activities into school or community youth programs.

4.3 Supporting Urban Conservation

- **Invasive Species Management:** Collaborate with local authorities to remove invasive plants while educating the public on their uses.
- **Pollinator Gardens:** Plant spaces that support pollinators and include edible plants for both wildlife and foragers.
- **Cleanup Events:** Combine foraging with environmental

cleanup efforts to restore and enhance green spaces.

---

5. Sharing the Bounty

One of the most rewarding aspects of urban foraging is sharing the fruits of your labor with others. This can take many forms, from gifting homemade treats to hosting communal meals.

5.1 Food Sharing Events

- **Potlucks:** Organize a potluck where each participant brings a dish made with foraged ingredients.
- **Cooking Nights:** Host a cooking event where attendees prepare and enjoy a meal together using their foraged finds.
- **Foraged Feasts:** Celebrate seasonal abundance with a feast highlighting wild ingredients.

5.2 Bartering and Gifting

- **Bartering:** Exchange surplus foraged goods with friends, neighbors, or local businesses. For example, trade wild herbs for homemade bread or fresh eggs.
- **Gifting:** Share jams, syrups, or teas made from foraged

ingredients as thoughtful, sustainable gifts.

5.3 Supporting Food Security

- **Donations:** Contribute excess foraged goods to community kitchens or food banks, helping to address food insecurity.
- **Education:** Teach others how to forage as a cost-effective way to supplement their diets.

6. Building Awareness and Advocacy

Urban foraging communities can play a vital role in raising awareness about sustainability, biodiversity, and food systems. By advocating for these issues, foragers contribute to broader societal change.

6.1 Educating the Public

- Host talks or presentations at libraries, schools, or community centers to share the benefits and ethics of foraging.
- Create educational materials, such as brochures or videos, to distribute in local neighborhoods.

6.2 Influencing Policy

- Advocate for policies that protect urban green spaces and allow responsible foraging.
- Work with local governments to establish designated foraging zones or guidelines.

6.3 Promoting Biodiversity

- Highlight the importance of wild plants in urban ecosystems.
- Encourage planting native species in backyards and public spaces to support foraging and conservation.

Urban foraging is more than a personal endeavor; it is a powerful tool for building community and fostering a deeper connection to the environment. By collaborating with others, sharing resources, and engaging in collective action, foragers can amplify their impact, creating a network of individuals united by their love for nature and sustainable living.

Chapter 10: Beyond Food: Foraging for Medicine and Crafting

Foraging is most often associated with food, but the potential uses of wild plants extend far beyond the dinner table. Across cultures and centuries, people have relied on the natural world not just for sustenance but also for healing and creativity. The art of foraging for medicinal and crafting purposes connects us to ancient traditions, inspires innovation, and fosters a deeper appreciation for the resources around us. This chapter will guide you through the exciting possibilities of using foraged materials for health and handmade creations, offering practical advice, detailed examples, and ethical considerations.

1. Foraging for Medicine

Many common wild plants have medicinal properties that can be used to support health and well-being. While modern medicine has largely supplanted these traditional remedies, they remain a valuable resource for natural health practices.

1.1 The Basics of Herbal Medicine

Herbal medicine involves using plant materials to promote health, prevent illness, or treat specific ailments. Foragers can harness these properties by creating teas, tinctures, salves, and more.

- **Start Small:** Focus on a few easy-to-identify medicinal plants.
- **Research Thoroughly:** Understand the plant's uses, dosages, and contraindications.
- **Consult Experts:** Seek guidance from herbalists or reliable references to ensure safe practices.

1.2 Common Medicinal Plants

1.2.1 Stinging Nettle (Urtica dioica)

- **Uses:** Anti-inflammatory, diuretic, and rich in iron and vitamins.
- **Preparation:** Make nettle tea by steeping dried leaves in hot water. Use fresh leaves in poultices for skin irritations.

1.2.2 Yarrow (Achillea millefolium)

- **Uses:** Wound healing, fever reduction, and digestive support.

- **Preparation:** Infuse dried yarrow flowers in oil for salves or brew a tea for colds and fevers.

1.2.3 Elderflower and Elderberries (Sambucus spp.)

- **Uses:** Boosts immunity, reduces cold symptoms, and promotes healthy skin.
- **Preparation:** Use elderflowers in soothing teas or make elderberry syrup as a natural remedy for colds.

1.2.4 Plantain (Plantago spp.)

- **Uses:** Soothes skin irritations, reduces inflammation, and aids in wound healing.
- **Preparation:** Crush fresh leaves into a poultice for insect bites or minor wounds.

1.2.5 Dandelion (Taraxacum officinale)

- **Uses:** Supports liver health, acts as a diuretic, and aids digestion.
- **Preparation:** Make dandelion root tea or tincture to promote liver detoxification.

1.3 Creating Simple Remedies

1.3.1 Teas and Infusions

- **Steps:**
    1. Wash and dry foraged herbs.
    2. Steep 1-2 teaspoons of dried herbs (or 2-3 teaspoons fresh) in a cup of hot water for 10-15 minutes.
    3. Strain and enjoy warm or cold.

1.3.2 Tinctures

- **Steps:**
    1. Fill a jar with chopped fresh or dried herbs.
    2. Cover with alcohol (vodka or brandy) and seal tightly.
    3. Store in a dark place for 4-6 weeks, shaking occasionally.
    4. Strain and store in amber bottles.

1.3.3 Salves

- **Steps:**
    1. Infuse herbs in oil (e.g., olive or coconut oil) over low heat.

2. Strain and mix with melted beeswax.
3. Pour into tins or jars and allow to cool.

---

2. Foraging for Crafting

The beauty and versatility of foraged materials make them ideal for a wide range of crafting projects. From creating natural dyes to weaving baskets, urban and wild landscapes offer an abundance of resources for artistic expression.

2.1 Gathering Crafting Materials

- **Sustainability:** Collect only what you need and leave enough for regeneration and wildlife.
- **Quality:** Choose materials that are fresh and undamaged. Avoid plants exposed to pollutants.
- **Tools:** Bring gloves, scissors, and baskets to gather and transport your finds.

2.2 Popular Crafting Materials and Their Uses

2.2.1 Willow Branches

- **Uses:** Basket weaving, wreaths, and decorative structures.
- **Tips:** Harvest in late winter or early spring when the

branches are most pliable.

2.2.2 Pinecones and Acorns

- **Uses:** Seasonal decorations, garlands, or centerpieces.
- **Tips:** Bake collected items at a low temperature to eliminate pests.

2.2.3 Bark (e.g., Birch or Cedar)

- **Uses:** Natural paper, container liners, or fire starters.
- **Tips:** Harvest fallen bark to avoid harming trees.

2.2.4 Wildflowers

- **Uses:** Pressed flower art, potpourri, or botanical prints.
- **Tips:** Collect on dry days and press flowers immediately for best results.

2.2.5 Nutshells and Seed Pods

- **Uses:** Jewelry, mobiles, or natural toys.
- **Tips:** Clean and dry thoroughly to prevent mold.

2.3 Crafting Projects

2.3.1 Natural Dyes

- **Ingredients:** Onion skins (yellow), blackberries (purple), nettles (green), and acorns (brown).

- **Steps:**
    1. Boil plant material in water to extract color.
    2. Strain and use the dye bath for fabrics or paper.

2.3.2 Foraged Wreaths

- **Materials:** Willow branches, evergreen boughs, pinecones, and berries.
- **Steps:**
    1. Shape flexible branches into a circle and secure with twine.
    2. Decorate with other materials using wire or glue.

2.3.3 Pressed Flower Art

- **Materials:** Wildflowers, heavy books, and parchment paper.
- **Steps:**
    1. Arrange flowers between parchment sheets.
    2. Place in a heavy book and leave for 1-2 weeks.
    3. Use pressed flowers for cards, bookmarks, or framed art.

2.3.4 Herb Bundles and Sachets

- **Materials:** Lavender, rosemary, or mint.
- **Steps:**
    1. Bundle herbs with twine for smudging sticks.
    2. Sew small sachets and fill them with dried herbs for drawer fresheners.

---

3. Combining Food, Medicine, and Crafting

Foraging provides a holistic way to integrate nature into every aspect of life. Combining its uses for food, medicine, and crafting creates opportunities for innovation and sustainability.

3.1 Seasonal Themes

- **Spring:** Create herbal teas, flower wreaths, and tinctures.
- **Summer:** Host wildflower pressing workshops and elderflower cordial-making events.
- **Autumn:** Craft acorn flour pancakes and decorate with foraged nuts and berries.
- **Winter:** Make pine needle tea and weave evergreen wreaths.

3.2 Sharing and Teaching

- Organize community workshops that explore the multiple uses of a single plant, such as crafting with willow and making willow bark tea.
- Host events where participants can forage together and create something meaningful from their finds.

Foraging for medicine and crafting transforms the way we interact with the natural world. These practices encourage mindfulness, creativity, and a deeper connection to the resources around us, proving that the value of foraged materials extends far beyond the plate.

Conclusion: Becoming an Urban Forager

Becoming an urban forager is not merely about learning to identify edible plants or crafting remedies from wildflowers; it's about embracing a lifestyle that reconnects us with nature in the midst of bustling cityscapes. It is a practice that challenges us to rethink our relationship with the land, our communities, and ourselves. As cities grow and the natural world adapts to urbanization, foraging becomes an act of resilience, creativity, and sustainability. This chapter will guide you through the final steps of your journey to becoming an urban forager, offering insights into the philosophy, ethics, and transformative power of this practice.

---

1. A Philosophy Rooted in Connection

At its core, urban foraging is about connection—to nature, to the seasons, and to the resources we often take for granted. By venturing into parks, alleyways, and untamed corners of the city, foragers witness the resilience of nature firsthand. Dandelions sprouting through cracks in the pavement or elderberries ripening in forgotten lots are reminders of nature's persistence and generosity.

1.1 Rethinking Urban Landscapes

- Cities are often seen as spaces devoid of nature, dominated by concrete and glass. Foraging reframes this perspective, revealing the abundance hidden in plain sight.
- Every neglected patch of soil or overlooked green space becomes an opportunity for discovery, fostering a sense of wonder and gratitude.

1.2 Reconnecting with the Seasons

- Foraging ties us to the rhythms of the seasons, encouraging mindfulness and anticipation. The arrival of spring greens, the abundance of summer berries, the rich harvest of autumn nuts and roots, and the quiet treasures of winter offer a continuous cycle of discovery.
- This seasonal awareness nurtures a deeper appreciation for the natural world and its gifts.

---

2. The Ethical Urban Forager

Ethics are paramount in foraging. As urban foragers, we must balance our desire to harvest with the responsibility to protect and preserve the ecosystems that sustain us. Ethical foraging ensures that this practice remains sustainable and respectful.

2.1 Harvesting with Care

- Always take only what you need, leaving enough for wildlife and regeneration.
- Focus on invasive or overabundant species to minimize ecological disruption.

2.2 Respecting Regulations and Property

- Familiarize yourself with local laws governing foraging. Public parks, private properties, and conservation areas may have specific rules.
- Seek permission when foraging on private land and respect any restrictions.

2.3 Educating Others

- Share knowledge about ethical practices with fellow foragers and the community.
- Lead by example, demonstrating sustainable and respectful harvesting methods.

3. Transforming the Way We Consume

Foraging has the power to reshape our consumption habits, encouraging a shift from dependency on industrial food systems to a more mindful and resourceful approach.

3.1 Reducing Food Waste

- Foraging teaches us to value what is often dismissed as weeds or waste. Wild greens like purslane and chickweed, commonly overlooked, become nutritious and delicious additions to our diets.
- By using every part of a plant—roots, leaves, flowers—foragers maximize the potential of each harvest.

3.2 Embracing Creativity in the Kitchen

- Foraged ingredients inspire culinary experimentation. Dandelion fritters, elderflower cordial, and nettle soup are just a few examples of how wild foods can elevate our meals.
- This creativity extends to preservation methods, such as drying, fermenting, or pickling, allowing foraged goods to be enjoyed year-round.

3.3 Supporting Local Ecosystems

- By focusing on invasive species and promoting the use of native plants, urban foragers contribute to biodiversity and ecological health.
- This mindful approach fosters a harmonious relationship between humans and the natural world.

---

4. Building Community Through Foraging

Foraging is not just a personal journey; it is a communal activity that brings people together through shared experiences and collective learning.

4.1 Creating Networks

- Join or form local foraging groups to share knowledge, organize walks, and host events.
- Online communities and social media platforms provide additional spaces for connection and resource sharing.

4.2 Hosting Educational Workshops

- Teach others about the joys and ethics of urban foraging through workshops or guided walks.
- Collaborate with schools, community centers, or environmental organizations to reach a wider audience.

4.3 Sharing the Bounty

- Host potlucks or foraged feasts to celebrate seasonal abundance.
- Barter or gift surplus finds to foster a spirit of generosity and sustainability.

5. The Transformative Power of Urban Foraging

Foraging transforms not just our relationship with the natural world but also how we see ourselves and our place within it. It is a practice of empowerment, resilience, and mindfulness.

5.1 Empowerment Through Knowledge

- Learning to identify, harvest, and use wild plants equips foragers with practical skills and confidence.
- This self-sufficiency is particularly empowering in times of economic uncertainty or environmental challenges.

5.2 Cultivating Resilience

- Urban foraging teaches adaptability and resourcefulness, qualities that extend beyond the practice itself.
- By embracing what the urban landscape offers, foragers develop a deeper sense of agency and resilience.

5.3 Practicing Mindfulness

- The act of foraging requires presence and attentiveness—to the plants, the environment, and the moment.
- This mindfulness fosters a sense of peace and gratitude, transforming foraging into a meditative practice.

---

6. Looking to the Future

As urbanization continues to reshape our world, foraging offers a pathway to sustainability, creativity, and community. The skills and mindset cultivated through foraging are more relevant than ever, providing tools to navigate the challenges of modern life.

6.1 Advocating for Green Spaces

- Urban foragers can play a role in advocating for the preservation and expansion of green spaces.
- Engaging with policymakers, participating in conservation efforts, and raising awareness about the value of wild plants are ways to contribute.

6.2 Inspiring the Next Generation

- Passing on the knowledge and philosophy of foraging to younger generations ensures its survival and growth.
- Encourage children to explore, learn, and appreciate the natural world through hands-on experiences.

6.3 Integrating Foraging into Urban Design

- Imagine cities designed with edible landscapes, where public spaces are filled with fruit trees, wild herbs, and community gardens.
- Urban foragers can collaborate with planners and designers to create environments that support both people and biodiversity.

Becoming an urban forager is a journey that goes beyond collecting wild plants. It is a lifestyle that invites us to see abundance where others see scarcity, to build community where others see isolation, and to find harmony where others see chaos. By embracing the philosophy, ethics, and transformative potential of foraging, we become not just foragers of food but stewards of our cities and the natural world.

Appendices

The appendices serve as a practical, resource-rich conclusion to this book, offering additional tools and references to deepen your foraging journey. These sections are designed to be quick reference guides, providing useful information for beginners and seasoned foragers alike. You'll find plant identification tips, a glossary of foraging terms, legal guidelines, seasonal charts, and recommendations for further reading and exploration.

Appendix A: Quick Reference Plant Identification Guide

Accurate plant identification is a cornerstone of safe and successful foraging. Use this guide to quickly distinguish common edible plants from their toxic lookalikes.

1. Dandelion (Taraxacum officinale)

- **Characteristics:**
    - Bright yellow flowers with multiple thin petals.
    - Deeply toothed leaves forming a basal rosette.
    - Milky sap when stems are broken.
- **Toxic Lookalike:** Catsear (Hypochaeris radicata).
    - **Difference:** Catsear has hairy leaves and branched

flower stems.

2. Stinging Nettle (Urtica dioica)

- **Characteristics:**
    - Serrated, heart-shaped leaves with fine stinging hairs.
    - Opposite leaf arrangement on square stems.
- **Toxic Lookalike:** Dead Nettle (Lamium purpureum).
    - **Difference:** Dead nettle lacks stinging hairs and has purple-tinted leaves.

3. Wild Garlic (Allium ursinum)

- **Characteristics:**
    - Broad, lance-shaped leaves with a garlic scent.
    - Clusters of white star-shaped flowers.
- **Toxic Lookalike:** Lily of the Valley (Convallaria majalis).
    - **Difference:** Lily of the Valley lacks the garlic scent and has bell-shaped flowers.

Appendix B: Glossary of Foraging Terms

Understanding the language of foraging will enhance your ability to follow guides and communicate with other foragers.

- **Basal Rosette:** A circular arrangement of leaves at the base of a plant.
- **Deciduous:** Plants that shed their leaves annually.
- **Herbaceous:** Plants with soft, non-woody stems.
- **Infusion:** A method of extracting plant compounds by steeping in hot water.
- **Mycelium:** The vegetative part of fungi, consisting of fine white filaments.
- **Node:** The part of a plant stem from which leaves or branches grow.
- **Perennial:** Plants that live for more than two years, often regrowing each season.
- **Tincture:** An extract made by soaking plant material in alcohol.

Appendix C: Legal and Ethical Foraging Guidelines

Before you set out, it's important to understand the legal and ethical considerations of foraging.

1. General Legal Guidelines

- **Public Lands:** Check local laws for specific regulations regarding foraging in parks, forests, and greenways.
- **Private Property:** Always seek permission from landowners before foraging.
- **Protected Plants:** Familiarize yourself with species that are protected or endangered in your region.

2. Ethical Foraging Practices

- Take only what you need and leave enough for the plant's regeneration and for wildlife.
- Focus on invasive species to help restore balance to local ecosystems.
- Use tools to minimize damage, such as scissors for cutting greens and knives for roots.

Appendix D: Seasonal Foraging Calendar

This chart provides a quick overview of what to forage throughout the year.

Season	Common Finds	Best Use
Spring	Dandelion greens, wild garlic, nettles	Salads, soups, teas
Summer	Purslane, elderflowers, blackberries	Fresh dishes, syrups, jams
Autumn	Mushrooms, acorns, rosehips	Stews, flour, teas
Winter	Pine needles, wintercress, dried berries	Teas, garnishes, preserved foods

Appendix E: Tools and Equipment Checklist

Ensure you're well-prepared for foraging adventures with this comprehensive equipment list.

1. Identification Tools

- Field guides specific to your region.
- Plant and mushroom identification apps (e.g., PictureThis, iNaturalist).

- Magnifying glass for examining small plant features.

2. Harvesting Tools

- Pruners or scissors for cutting stems and leaves.
- Trowel for digging roots.
- Gloves to handle prickly or stinging plants.

3. Carrying and Storage

- Woven basket or cloth bag for harvested plants.
- Paper bags for mushrooms to prevent spoilage.
- Small containers for delicate berries.

4. Safety and Comfort

- Notebook and pen for recording finds.
- Water bottle and snacks.
- First-aid kit for minor cuts or stings.

Appendix F: Conversion Charts and Measurements

Foragers often work with fresh ingredients that need to be measured and processed. These charts simplify the process.

1. Fresh to Dried Herb Conversion

- 1 tablespoon fresh herbs = 1 teaspoon dried herbs.

2. Volume to Weight Conversions

- 1 cup of fresh greens = 30 grams (approx.).
- 1 cup of berries = 150 grams (approx.).

3. Liquid Measurements

- 1 tablespoon = 15 milliliters.
- 1 cup = 240 milliliters.

Appendix G: Resources for Further Exploration

Expand your foraging knowledge and skills with these recommended books, websites, and organizations.

1. Books

- *The Forager's Harvest* by Samuel Thayer.
- *Edible Wild Plants: Wild Foods from Dirt to Plate* by John Kallas.
- *Mushrooms Demystified* by David Arora.

2. Websites

- Wild Food UK: Comprehensive plant guides and foraging tips.
- Forager's Library: An extensive database of wild edibles.

3. Organizations

- **North American Mycological Association:** Resources and events for mushroom enthusiasts.
- **Slow Food USA:** Advocates for sustainable food practices, including foraging.

Appendix H: Common Foraging Mistakes and How to Avoid Them

Even experienced foragers can make mistakes. Learning from these common errors will help you stay safe and successful.

1. Misidentification

- **Mistake:** Confusing edible plants with toxic lookalikes.
- **Solution:** Cross-reference multiple sources and consult experts when in doubt.

2. Overharvesting

- **Mistake:** Taking too much from a single area.
- **Solution:** Follow the "10% rule" and leave enough for the ecosystem.

3. Ignoring Contamination

- **Mistake:** Foraging in polluted or treated areas.
- **Solution:** Avoid areas near roads, factories, or sprayed fields. Test soil if necessary.

4. Improper Storage

- **Mistake:** Allowing fresh finds to spoil.
- **Solution:** Process or preserve your harvest promptly using drying, freezing, or pickling methods.

These appendices are designed to be a lasting resource, equipping you with the tools and knowledge to forage confidently and responsibly. Keep them handy as you embark on your urban foraging adventures, and let them guide you to deeper connections with nature and the community around you.

Printed in Great Britain
by Amazon

c730efe3-561d-429f-87f1-cbccecbe80beR01